Introvert:

A Scientific Explanation and Guide to an Introvert's Mind

Table of Contents

Table of Contents 1
Introduction 3
Chapter 1: What Is An Introvert? 5
Chapter 2: A Short History of Introverts 10
Chapter 3: What Does Science Say About Introverts? 17
Chapter 4: How Are Introvert Genes Different? 19
Chapter 5: How Are Introvert Brains Different? 21
Chapter 6: Do Introverts Think Differently? 23
Chapter 7: How Do Introverts Behave Differently? 24
Chapter 8: Are Introverts Less Happy Than Extraverts? 26
Chapter 9: Introverts In The Real World 30
Chapter 10: What Characteristics Do Successful Introverts Have In Common? .. 34
Chapter 11: Where Can Things Get Problematic for Introverts in a Social Society? 36
Chapter 12: So How Can Introverts Win? 39
Chapter 13: What Does The Future Hold for Introverts? 42
Chapter 14: Can Society Change? Can Introverts Change? And Should They? 43
Conclusion 46

© Copyright 2016 by Madge Falco - All rights reserved.

This document is geared towards providing exact and reliable information in regards to the topic and issue covered. The publication is sold with the idea that the publisher is not required to render accounting, officially permitted, or otherwise qualified services. If advice is necessary, legal or professional, a practiced individual in the profession should be ordered from a Declaration of Principles which was accepted and approved equally by a Committee of the American Bar Association and a Committee of Publishers and Associations.

In no way is it legal to reproduce, duplicate, or transmit any part of this document in either electronic means or in printed format. Recording of this publication is strictly prohibited and any storage of this document is not allowed without written permission from the publisher. All rights are reserved.

The information provided herein is stated to be truthful and consistent, in that any liability, in terms of inattention or otherwise, by any usage or abuse of any policies, processes, or directions contained herein is the solitary and utter responsibility of the recipient reader. Under no circumstances will any legal responsibility or blame be held against the publisher for any reparation, damages, or monetary loss due to the information herein, either directly or indirectly.

Respective authors own all copyrights not held by the publisher.

The information herein is offered for informational purposes solely, and is universal as so. The presentation of the information is without contract or any type of guarantee assurance.

The trademarks that are used are without any consent from, and the publication of the trademark is without permission or backing by, the trademark owner. All trademarks and brands within this book are for clarifying purposes only, are owned by the owners themselves, and are not affiliated with this document.

Introduction

It's tough to be an introvert in an extravert world.

It can also be a huge advantage to be an introvert in an extravert world.

Whether you see introversion as an advantage or disadvantage depends largely on your lens.

Fascination with introverts, what makes them tick, and how they function in the world, has hit an all-time high, most likely because introverts are finally being studied, understood, and validated in a major way.

Because they tend to prefer quiet, deep thought, and solitude, and to shy away from self-aggrandizement and social situations, introverts also tend to appear mysterious and standoffish to the casual extravert observer. This has led many introverts to feel misunderstood and misjudged.

Much of modern society, especially in the United States, favors the bold, assertive, sociable extravert over the quiet introvert. So introverts have grown up in this society thinking there was something wrong with them. That they were abnormal or anti-social.

Thankfully, recent attention has shed light on the misunderstood introvert.

It has revealed that introversion is as valid a way of being as extraversion. It has revealed that there are real physical and biological differences between introverts and extraverts that may explain the differences in their behavior. And it has revealed that introverts have qualities that are just as valuable as those of extraverts…qualities which can help introverts thrive, even in an extravert world.

What This Book Is All About

In the first eight chapters, we will explore the fascinating inner world of the introvert.

We will explore the history of introverts and the many psychological models of personality (of which introversion is one dimension).

We will also explore all the fascinating science behind introverts, to find out what makes them tick: genetically, physically, and behaviorally.

And we will try to answer the ultimate question: Are introverts unhappier than extraverts?

In the last six chapters, we will look at the unique qualities of introverts. How can their unique traits help them succeed? And how do their unique traits trip them up?

We will examine successful introverts of the past and present and look ahead to see what place introverts have in shaping society's future.

Hopefully, you will come away with a basic social and scientific understanding of what introversion really is.

If you are not an introvert, you will come away with a better understanding of the inner workings of the introvert mind.

And if you are an introvert, you should come away with a better appreciation of who you are.

Let's begin.

Chapter 1: What Is An Introvert?

In the 1960s, Isabel Myers, known for the Myers-Briggs personality test, estimated that introverts made up about 25% of the population of the United States.[1] For a long time, this percentage was generally accepted.

Introverts believed they were in the minority. And little wonder that they did, considering that introverts are not valued in America's very extraverted culture. We live in a culture that values boldness and assertiveness.

So introverts have a tendency to believe that their more noticeable, extraverted family, friends, neighbors, and colleagues make up the majority. In fact, you will still find people throwing around 25% as the low end of the range when they describe the percentage of introverts in the United States.

However, a more accurate measure, based on a Myers-Briggs random sample released in 1998, shows that the United States is split almost 50/50 between introverts and extraverts.[2]

A more recently published study, "Estimated Frequencies of the Types in the United States Population," offers the following ranges for introversion/extraversion: Introverts – 47-55% and Extraverts – 45-53%.[3] In her book, "Quiet: The Power of Introverts in a World That Can't Stop Talking," Susan Cain estimates the number of introverts to be anywhere from one-third to one-half of the U.S. population.[4]

Considering that about half of the country are introverts, we might find it helpful to understand them. Specifically:

- Who are they?
- What are the major psychological theories behind this personality trait?
- What does science say about introversion?
- What are the strengths and weaknesses of introverts?
- Can introverts be successful in an extravert society?

---

[1] http://introvertzone.com/ratio-of-introverts

[2] Myers, I. B., McCaulley, M. H., Quenk, N. L., & Hammer, A. L. (1998). *MBTI Manual: A guide to the development and use of the Myers-Briggs Type Indicator* (3rd Ed.). Palo Alto, CA: Consulting Psychologists Press. Actual percentages were 50.7% Introverts and 49.3% Extraverts.

[3] https://www.capt.org/mbti-assessment/estimated-frequencies.htm

[4] Cain, Susan. *Quiet: The Power of Introverts in a World That Can't Stop Talking*. Broadway Books. (2013).

- What does the future hold for introverts?

What is an Introvert?

There is no doubt that introverts are very popular these days.

A brief Internet search on introverts brings up 4,480,000 pages written and published online in 2016 alone.

Susan Cain's 2013 book, "Quiet: The Power of Introverts in a World That Can't Stop Talking," spawned an entire subcategory of books on introversion. You can go into any bookstore or search Amazon and find books on everything from "Introverts in Love" to "Introvert Leaders That Run The World."

But there seems to be some confusion on just what constitutes an introvert. Many of these articles will equate shyness or social anxiety with introversion. Just as many others will tell you that, no, introversion is NOT the same thing as shyness, social anxiety, or awkwardness at parties.

There's even an amusing article in the Scientific American that will tell you that, no, Kanye West probably isn't an introvert so much as a narcissist.[5]

Shyness and social awkwardness on one hand. Narcissism and extreme self-centeredness on the other. And introverts, somewhere in the middle.

So what, exactly, is an introvert?

The Dictionary Definition

Let's start with the dictionary definition:

> Introvert: 1. A shy person, 2. Psychology. A person characterized by concern primarily with his or her own thoughts and feelings (as opposed to an extravert).

Sadly, even the dictionary definition reinforces a stereotype that "introvert" is interchangeable with "shy person," or someone who is anxious in social situations, or even antisocial. None of these, however, are true.

Can an introvert can be shy? Sure. But an introvert can also be confident, assertive, and friendly. Introversion has little to do with shyness or social awkwardness.

---

[5] http://blogs.scientificamerican.com/beautiful-minds/23-signs-youe28099re-secretly-a-narcissist-masquerading-as-a-sensitive-introvert/

The Psychological Definition

Introverts have certainly been around since the dawn of history. But the recognition of "introvert" as a key dimension of personality is a fairly modern discovery, starting in the 1920s with Swiss psychologist Carl Jung.

Jung, the father of the modern psychological definition of introversion and extraversion, believed that introverts view the world through a subjective lens (of their inner thoughts, dreams, and feelings) and extraverts view the world through an objective lens (through interaction with the world itself).

Jung believed that introverts got their psychic energy from their inner world, while extraverts derive theirs from interacting with the outer world. Introverts recharge their mental energy in solitude, in spending time with their own thoughts, in their inner world. Extraverts, on the other hand, recharge their mental energy by being among other people, being active, or otherwise interacting with the outer world.

To be an introvert means that your focus is inward rather than outward. To be an introvert means that you are inner-directed, rather than outward-directed.

To be an introvert means that your primary motivations come from your own thoughts, feelings, and values, rather than being primarily motivated by outside opinion, attention or validation.

Which isn't to say that an introvert is more selfish or self-centered than the extravert. It just means they get their energy from within themselves, rather than from the outer world as extraverts do.

Later psychological frameworks focused less on where the introvert or extravert gets their mental energy (since "mental energy" can't be tested or measured) and more on the individual facets that make up introversion: Warmth, Gregariousness, Assertiveness, Activity, Excitement-Seeking, and Positive Emotion.[6]

The more recent models of personality view introversion not just as a single quality, but a complex combination of qualities.[7] So the higher a person scores on introversion, the lower that person will score on measures related to how

---

[6] Costa, P. T., Jr., & McCrae, R. R. (1992). *NEO PI-R professional manual*. Odessa, FL: Psychological Assessment Resources, Inc.

[7] See, for example, the NEO-PI-R personality inventory, with its 6 facets of introversion, discussed in Chapter 2; Costa, P. T., Jr., & McCrae, R. R. (1992). *NEO PI-R professional manual*. Odessa, FL: Psychological Assessment Resources, Inc.

warm, gregarious, assertive, active, excitement-seeking, and positive that person is.

But these qualities are not absolutes. They are not either-or propositions, and different introverts will show differing levels for each quality.

In fact, the whole concept of introverts versus extraverts is a continuum, a spectrum where we may fall closer to the introvert side, closer to the extravert side, or somewhere in the middle.

Qualities of an Introvert

Definitions are useful, but when describing any dimension of personality, perhaps the best way to define an introvert is by listing the qualities that are more common to introverts. Introverts are:

- Deep thinkers
- Thoughtful
- Reflective
- Self-aware
- Self-motivated
- Independent
- Observant
- Focused
- Quiet

Introverts tend to:

- Expend energy in social situations
- Recharge in solitude
- React slowly
- Think deeply
- Prefer routine
- Avoid risk-taking
- Dislike surprise and change
- Form deep, rather than superficial, relationships

This is by no means a complete list of introvert qualities, but it should give you a more complete sense of what an introvert is.

The Introversion-Extraversion Spectrum

The truth is, while we may identify as either an introvert or an extravert, it is more accurate to say that most of us fall somewhere in between. We may tend more towards introversion or extraversion, but no one is purely one or the other.

Even Carl Jung, the psychologist who first conceived of introversion and extraversion as key dimensions of personality said "There is no such thing as a pure introvert or extravert. Such a person would be in a lunatic asylum."[8]

In fact, there are even ambiverts, who fall near the midpoint of the spectrum. Ambiverts generally feel comfortable and energized by social situations, but may still require alone time.

So while we may identify more as introverts or extraverts, the concept of introversion is a lot more fluid than you might think.

---

8 Evans, Richard I., Jung, C.G., and Jones, Alfred Ernest. Conversations with Carl Jung & Reactions from Ernest Jones, Princeton: D. Van Nostrand Company, Inc. (1964)

Chapter 2: A Short History of Introverts

Despite the renewed interest in introverts in recent years, introversion – as a word – actually has a long history going back to the 1660s. As a psychological concept, it has been around since the early 1900s.

This makes sense. After all, introversion is nothing new. The ancient Greeks may have been the first to try to classify people by personality, but the psychological concept of introversion started with Carl Jung. Its roots can be traced through the evolution of psychology's understanding of personality, across the different models of personality, and down to continuing research in the field of personality today.

The Ancient Greeks

Theophrastus. Possibly the first man to try to catalogue people according to their personalities, Theophrastus was a Greek philosopher and student of both Plato and Aristotle who lived from 371 to 287 BC. While he had many interests (he is also known for being the "father of botany"), he made his mark on the study of personality by writing his book *Characters,* which included descriptions of 30 "moral types."[9]

Hippocrates & Galen. Considered the father of medicine and the creator of the Hippocratic Oath that doctors still take to this day, Hippocrates lived from 460 to 370 B.C. His successor, Galen, lived from 129 to 200 A.D. Both men believed there were four "humors" or temperaments: choleric, sanguine, melancholic, and phlegmatic.[10] The choleric and sanguine temperaments were more excitable. The melancholic and phlegmatic temperaments were closer to what we would consider introverts today.

Hippocrates and Galen also believed that these temperaments were caused or influenced by a person's bodily fluids. They argued that the sanguine temperament, for example, was influenced by the blood. While not exactly accurate, they may have been the first to attempt to explore a biological explanation for personality differences.

It was not until 2,000 years later, however, that science would introduce introversion as a personality trait.

---

[9] https://en.wikipedia.org/wiki/Theophrastus#Characters

[10] https://en.wikipedia.org/wiki/Four_temperaments#Sanguine

Carl Jung's Concept of Introversion/Extraversion

While it has likely always existed as a dimension of personality, the term *introversion* wasn't "discovered" until Swiss psychologist Carl Jung coined it in the 1920s.

Jung, the father of analytical psychology, was the first modern psychologist to advance the dichotomy of the introverted and extraverted personality types, which he introduced in his 1921 book, "Psychological Types."

Jung claimed that everyone was either an introvert or an extravert. As one author described it, by Jung's definition, introverts find fulfillment in the inner world of ideas and feelings, while extraverts find it by interacting with the outer world of people and environment.[11]

Psychologists would later come to see introversion-extraversion as a continuum, rather than two opposite extremes where we either fall to one side or the other, but Jung got the ball rolling.

Myers-Briggs Type Indicator

Carl Jung's concepts of introversion and extraversion eventually became the basis for the personality test that college students and job seekers are very familiar with: the Myers-Briggs Type Indicator (MBTI).

Katharine Briggs and her daughter, Isabel Briggs Meyers, constructed the MBTI to help people determine where they fell within four cognitive functions, including introversion-extraversion.

According to The Myers & Briggs Foundation website, it defines introversion-extraversion being based on one's "favorite world":

"Favorite world: Do you prefer to focus on the outer world or on your own inner world? This is called Extraversion (E) or Introversion (I)."[12]

According to this definition, extraverts would prefer the outer world and introverts would prefer the inner world.

The original test was published in 1944. While still used for academic and business purposes, the Myers-Briggs model was replaced by other models considered to be more accurate.

---

[11] Jung, C.G.. *Psychological Types*. (1921)

[12] http://www.myersbriggs.org/my-mbti-personality-type/mbti-basics/

Moving Toward a Deeper Understanding of Personality Traits

Gordon Allport. American psychologist Gordon Allport attempted to catalogue human personality by taking every adjective in the dictionary that could be applied to personality and systematically classifying it. What he ended up with was a list of 4,500 traits, which he organized into cardinal traits, central traits, and secondary traits.[13]

While his list of 4,500 traits was a little too cumbersome to be useful, it did inspire others to pare down the list to a more elegant and simplified understanding of human personality.

Raymond Cattell. British psychologist Raymond Cattell took Allport's list and narrowed it down to 16 dimensions of personality[14]:

1. Abstractedness
2. Warmth
3. Apprehension
4. Emotional Stability
5. Liveliness
6. Openness to Change
7. Perfectionism
8. Privateness
9. Intelligence
10. Rule Consciousness
11. Tension
12. Sensitivity
13. Social Boldness
14. Self-Reliance
15. Vigilance
16. Dominance

While his 16-dimension model is not used as he originally conceived it, many of the dimensions he named have made their way into later models of personality.

---

[13] https://www.boundless.com/psychology/textbooks/boundless-psychology-textbook/personality-16/trait-perspectives-on-personality-79/allport-s-cattell-s-and-eysenck-s-trait-theories-of-personality-310-12845/

[14] https://www.boundless.com/psychology/textbooks/boundless-psychology-textbook/personality-16/trait-perspectives-on-personality-79/allport-s-cattell-s-and-eysenck-s-trait-theories-of-personality-310-12845/

Hans Eysenck's "Stimulation" Hypothesis and the Three Factor Model

A German-born psychologist who spent his career in the UK, Hans Eysenck contributed greatly to the progress of the psychological understanding of personality.
In his 1967 book "Dimensions of Personality," he described personality as containing two dimensions: extraversion and neuroticism. He added a third dimension to his model in the 1970s: psychoticism.

According to his Three Factor Model, any given individual can score high or low on any given dimension. For example, one might be low in extraversion (in other words, be an introvert), high in neuroticism and low in psychoticism.

In addition to proposing the three dimensions, he also attempted to explain why certain people had certain personalities. In explaining introversion-extraversion, Eysenck suggested that individuals were either more or less extraverted because of cortical arousal in the brain.

He stated "introverts are characterized by higher levels of activity than extraverts and so are chronically more cortically aroused than extraverts."[15] Because of the higher levels of arousal in introvert brains, it followed that introverts sought less stimulation: less social interaction, less activity, more solitude and quiet.

This was one of the earliest attempts at explaining the cause of personality by looking at biology. It also gave scientists a theory they could actually measure and test through controlled experiments.

The Big Five Model

Although the concepts behind it evolved steadily from the 1930s to the 1980s, a five-factor model of personality became widespread in the early 1980s. This model is based on the idea that there are five dimensions of the personality:

1. Openness to experience
2. Conscientiousness
3. Extraversion
4. Agreeableness
5. Neuroticism

You might have noticed that two of the dimensions in this "Big Five Model" – Extraversion and Neuroticism – were borrowed from Hans Eysenck's Three Factor Model. As with Eysenck's Three Factor Model, an individual could score

---

[15] Eysenck, Hans, Eysenck, M.W, *Personality and Individual Differences: A Natural Science Approach* (1985)

high or low on any one of the Big 5 personality traits, and the score for each trait was separate and independent from that person's scores for the other traits.

6 Facets of Introversion (NEO-PI-R Personality Test)

The acceptance of the Big Five Model of personality in the early 1980s led to the development of the NEO five-factor personality inventory in 1985 by Paul Costa and Robert McCrae, researchers at the National Institute on Aging. Originally, Costa and McCrae began researching only the factors Neuroticism (N), Extraversion (E), and Openness to Experience (O), with their Neuroticism-Extraversion-Openness Inventory (NEO-I). This inventory was extended to include two additional factors (Agreeableness and Conscientiousness) in 1985, leading to the five factor personality test known as the NEO Personality Inventory (NEO PI). This was later refined and renamed the NEO-PI-R (or Revised NEO Personality Inventory).

Costa and McCrae revised the NEO tests to include 6 facets within each of the Big 5 personality traits,[16] which ultimately resulted in the creation of 6 separate facets to introversion-extraversion. They concluded that since introverts vary from person to person in how they score on these different facets, there must be different variations and types of introverts.

The 6 facets of introversion/extraversion are:

1. Warmth
2. Gregariousness
3. Assertiveness
4. Activity
5. Excitement-Seeking
6. Positive Emotion

Warmth: This facet measures the ease or difficulty of getting to know someone, and whether individuals feel comfortable around people they don't know. People who score high on introversion tend to be hard to get to know initially, but can be quite comfortable around people they already know.

Gregariousness: This facet measures the ability and enthusiasm for being in social situations, including being around other people and meeting new people. People who score high on the introversion end of this facet tend to prefer solitude or quiet, and feel uncomfortable in large crowds.

Assertiveness: This facet measures the ability to express yourself to make sure your needs are being met. People who score high on introversion tend to not

---

[16] Costa, P. T., Jr., & McCrae, R. R. (1992). *NEO PI-R professional manual*. Odessa, FL: Psychological Assessment Resources, Inc.

speak up about their own needs, and will wait patiently while others are being helped first.

Activity: This facet measures a person's desire and inclination for living a high-paced lifestyle. Not surprisingly, introverts tend to prefer a less active, more relaxed lifestyle and they tend to react slowly to events.

Excitement-Seeking: This facet measures the need to be stimulated and to take risks. People who scored high on introversion tended to avoid excitement and risky behavior, preferring safety and quiet routine instead.

Positive Emotion: This facet measures the ease or difficulty of expressing happiness or joy. Interestingly, this facet does not measure whether one is actually happy but rather, whether they *express it* outwardly. People who score high on introversion can be happy, but they tend to keep it to themselves.

Studies have found the original five factor model of personality which the NEO-PI-R is based on (those factors being: Openness to experience, Conscientiousness, Extraversion, Agreeableness, and Neuroticism) to be true across a number of different cultures.[17] [18] [19] [20]

In fact, these studies showed that introverts who took the test over time would score differently at different points in their lives, showing that introversion is not a single, fixed personality trait.[21]

Recent Research on Introversion

Incremental refinements to, and variations of, the Big Five Model over the last 35 years reflect psychology's ongoing efforts to define introversion-extraversion in

---

[17] Trull, T. J.; Geary, D. C. (1997). "Comparison of the big-five factor structure across samples of Chinese and American adults". *Journal of Personality Assessment*. **69** (2): 324–341. doi:10.1207/s15327752jpa6902_6. PMID 9392894

[18] Lodhi, P. H., Deo, S., & Belhekar, V. M. (2002). The Five-Factor model of personality in Indian context: measurement and correlates. In R. R. McCrae & J. Allik (Eds.), *The Five-Factor model of personality across cultures* (pp. 227–248). N.Y.: Kluwer Academic Publisher

[19] McCrae, R. R. (2002). NEO-PI-R data from 36 cultures: Further Intercultural comparisons. In R. R. McCrae & J. Allik. (Eds.), *The Five-Factor model of personality across cultures* (pp. 105–125). New York: Kluwer Academic Publisher.

[20] Thompson, E.R. (2008). "Development and validation of an international English big-five mini-markers". *Personality and Individual Differences*. **45** (6): 542–548. doi:10.1016/j.paid.2008.06.013

[21] Terraciano, A., McCrae, R.R., Brant, L.J., & Costa P.R. (2005). Hierarchical linear modeling analyses of the NEO-PI-R Scales in the Baltimore Longitudinal Study of Aging. *Psychology and Aging*, (20)3, 493-506. doi: 10.1037/0082-7974.20.3.493

different ways. Some focused on social behavior, while others examined positive emotions, reputation, or evolution of behavior.

These variations include:

- Auke Tellegen and Niels Waller's *Big Seven*, which included the Big Five personality traits, as well as two more: Positive Valence and Negative Valence.[22] In this model, Positive Valence and Negative Valence refer to whether a person views himself or herself positively or negatively. As you might expect, a person with Positive Valence has a higher self-esteem than someone with Negative Valence.

- Robert Hogan's *Socioanalytic Theory*, which proposed that personality is the result of evolutionary adaptation to either get along or get ahead.[23]

- Michael Ashton and Kibeom Lee's *HEXACO* model of personality, which measures six factors: Honesty-Humility (H), Emotionality (E), Extraversion (X), Agreeableness (A), Conscientiousness (C), and Openness to Experience (E). The difference between this model and others is a factor which is unique to this model: Humility-Honesty.[24]

In recent years, researchers have been less interested in simply constructing more theories to explain and classify personality, and more focused on producing quantitative research that actually measures and tests differences between introverts and extraverts.

These studies include research examining:

- The genetics of introverts and extraverts
- The brain function of introverts and extraverts
- The temperament and behavior of introverts and extraverts
- Even whether extraverts are happier than introverts

---

[22] Tellegen, A., & Waller, N. G. (1987). Reexamining basic dimensions of natural language trait descriptors. Paper presented at the 95th annual meeting of the American Psychological Association, New York.

[23] Hogan, R. (1983). A socioanalytic theory of personality. In M. M. Page (Ed.), *1982 Nebraska Symposium on Motivation* (pp. 55–89). Lincoln: University of Nebraska Press.

[24] Lee, K.; Ashton, M.C. (2004). "The HEXACO Personality Inventory: A New Measure of the Major Dimensions of Personality". *Multivariate Behavioural Research*. **39**: 329–258. doi:10.1207/s15327906mbr3902_8.

The study of introversion is currently in a state of massive growth. New and innovative research is being conducted on a continuous basis, allowing us to improve our understanding of what it means to be an introvert. In the next chapter, we'll take a closer look at the science behind introverts, including some of these newer studies, and what we have discovered about introvert genetics, brains, behavior, and happiness.

Chapter 3: What Does Science Say About Introverts?

While all of the psychological theories on personality are interesting from an academic perspective, the practical questions have to be asked:

- Does the science support these theories?

- Have scientists found any physiological or biological differences between introverts and extraverts?

- Have they found genetic differences between introverts and extraverts? Have they found differences in the brains of introverts and extraverts?

- Have studies found marked differences in the way introverts and extraverts actually think, feel, and behave?

Over the past couple of decades, scientists have been busy trying to answer these questions, and have arrived at some interesting conclusions about introverts. On the other hand, during this same period, different studies have also produced conflicting results. Clearly, the final verdict on introverts is still far off in the future, but for now, let's take a look at what the experts have concluded about introverts and extraverts to date.

Studies Have Found Differences Between Introverts and Extraverts

Not surprisingly, experts have concluded that there are genetic, neurological, cognitive, and behavioral differences between introverts and extraverts:

Genetic: Studies have shown that there is a genetic component to introversion and extraversion. Like many aspects of our personalities, introversion is partially inherited from our parents.[25] While genetics can't fully explain a person's tendency towards being an introvert versus being an extravert, as discussed in the previous chapter, scientists have begun the work of identifying which genes are responsible for introversion.[26]

Biological & Cognitive: Eysenck claimed that introversion and extraversion can be explained by differing levels of arousal in the brain. Other studies, however, have confirmed that there are significant differences in the brains of

---

[25] Bouchard, J., Thomas J., & Loehlin, J.C. (2001). Genes, evolution and personality. *Behavior Genetics*, 31(3), 243-273

[26] Luo, X., Kranzler, H.R., Zuo, L., S., & Gelernter, J. (2007). Personality traits of agreeableness and extraversion are associated with adh4 variation. *Biological Psychiatry*, 61(5), 599-608.

introverts and extraverts. Specifically, by looking at blood flow and brain volume, these studies concluded that introverts and extraverts process incoming information in different parts of the brain.[27] [28]

Behavioral: According to some studies, introverts and extraverts have consistent differences in the way they behave, from the way they dress,[29] to the music they listen to,[30] to the way they decorate their offices.[31] But other studies have found that introverts and extraverts frequently exhibit behavior of the opposite type, with introverts sometimes behaving more like extraverts, and vice versa.[32] So introvert and extravert behavior may be more fluid than we imagine.

Happiness: Perhaps most interesting are the studies exploring the link between extraversion and happiness. Extraverts have been shown to have higher levels of happiness and self-esteem.[33] But does that necessarily mean that introverts are less happy? If so, why?

In the following chapters, we will take a look at how researchers have studied each type of difference listed above, and how those differences have deepened our understanding of introversion and extraversion.

---

[27] Johnson, DL; Wiebe, JS; Gold, SM; Andreasen, NC; Hichwa, RD; Watkins, GL; Boles Ponto, LL (1999). "Cerebral blood flow and personality: A positron emission tomography study". *The American Journal of Psychiatry*. 156 (2): 252-7. PMID 9989562.

[28] Forsman, L.J., de Manzano, O., Karabanov, A., Madison, G. & Ullen, F. (2012) Differences in regional brain volume related to the extraversion-introversion dimension—a voxel based morphometry study. *Neuroscience Research*, 72(1), 59-67

[29] Sharma, R. S. (1980). "Clothing behavior, personality, and values: A correlational study". *Psychological Studies*. 25 (2): 137–42.

[30] Rentfrow, Peter J.; Gosling, Samuel D. (2003). "The do re mi's of everyday life: The structure and personality correlates of music preferences". *Journal of Personality and Social Psychology*. 84 (6): 1236–56. doi:10.1037/0022-3514.84.6.1236. PMID 12793587.

[31] Gosling, S. (2008). *Snoop*. New York: Basic Books.

[32] Fleeson, W.; Gallagher, P. (2009). "The Implications of Big Five Standing for the Distribution of Trait Manifestation in Behavior: Fifteen Experience-Sampling Studies and a Meta-Analysis". *Journal of Personality and Social Psychology*. 87 (6): 1097–1114. doi:10.1037/a0016786.

[33] Pavot, William; Diener, Ed; Fujita, Frank. (1990). "Extraversion and happiness." *Personality and Individual Differences*. 11(12):1299-306. doi:10.1016/0191-8869(90)90157-M

Chapter 4: How Are Introvert Genes Different?

If you are an introvert, you may have inherited your introversion from your parents.

Scientists have found that several aspects of personality are inherited. Some have turned their attention towards introversion in order to figure out:

- How much of our introversion is explained by genes?
- What genes are responsible for introversion?

According to these studies, introversion or extraversion is "moderately heritable." One study found that introversion or extraversion could be accounted for 45-50% by genes.[34] In addition, studies on identical twins have found that genes may be 39-58% responsible for the tendency towards introversion or extraversion.[35] Another study found that several facets of the Big 5 personality dimensions could be accounted for by genetics.[36] So being an introvert may very well be more nature than nurture.

But genetics is not the whole story. According to a study by Bouchard & Loehlin, the effect of our genes lessens with age, and even the studies above concede that behavioral influences are at least partially responsible for introversion or extraversion. Therefore, while genetic influence may not be the only factor in determining whether we are introverts or extraverts, it is nonetheless a growing area of research.

Finally, while scientists believe something as complex as a personality trait will ultimately be attributable to several genes, some studies have suggested that specific, individual genes may have a direct impact on introversion. A 2007 study identified one possibility in the ADH4 gene.[37] The researchers in this study noted that strong associations had already been identified between the ADH4 gene and substance dependence (alcohol or drugs). They further observed that there were

---

[34] Bouchard, J., Thomas J., & Loehlin, J.C. (2001). Genes, evolution and personality. *Behavior Genetics*, 31(3), 243-273

[35] Tellegen, Auke; Lykken, David T.; Bouchard Jr, Thomas J.; Wilcox, Kimberly J.; Segal, NL; Rich, S (1988). "Personality similarity in twins reared apart and together". *Journal of Personality and Social Psychology*. **54** (6): 1031–9. doi:10.1037/0022-3514.54.6.1031. PMID 3397862.

[36] Jang, K.L., Livesly, W., Angleitner, A., Riemann, R., & Vernon, P.A. (2002). Genetic and environmental influences on the covariance of facets defining the domains of the five-factor model of personality. *Personality and Individual Differences*, 33(1), 83-101.

[37] Luo, X., Kranzler, H.R., Zuo, L., S., & Gelernter, J. (2007). Personality traits of agreeableness and extraversion are associated with adh4 variation. *Biological Psychiatry*, 61(5), 599-608.

specific personality traits also associated with substance dependence, and theorized that there might therefore be a link between the specific personality traits and the ADH4 gene.

The researchers in the ADH4 study used a five-factor personality test on 243 individuals with substance dependence (and 296 control subjects with no substance dependence). They also genotyped 7 markers of the ADH4 gene and 38 unrelated markers in these individuals. They found strong associations between the personality traits of agreeableness and extraversion and certain portions of the ADH4 gene, and concluded that there was a genetic basis for personality traits like extraversion.

There may come a day when scientists have mapped every gene associated with introversion. The wealth of existing research available today on the relationship between genes and introversion could revolutionize how we think about introversion in the years to come.

Chapter 5: How Are Introvert Brains Different?

As early as the 1960s, psychologist Hans Eysenck proposed that introverts are more cortically aroused in their brains than extraverts, leading them to seek out less stimulation.

Recent studies examining the physical structure of the brain have shown that there are, indeed, physical differences between the introvert and extravert brain which may explain the introvert personality. Those studies concluded that:

Introverts have more blood flow to certain portions of the brain involved in planning and problem-solving.

A study found that introverts have more blood flow to the frontal lobes and the thalamus. Extraverts, on the other hand, have more blood flow to other portions of the brain, which are highly associated with the physical senses and emotions.[38]

Introverts have greater brain volume in certain areas of the brain involved with inhibition and withdrawal.

Introverts have greater gray matter volume in their right prefrontal cortex and tempoparietal junction. They also have greater white matter volume overall. Extraverts, on the other hand, are associated with greater gray matter volume in the left prefrontal cortex.[39]

Extraverts are more sensitive to dopamine rewards.

Extraverts, on the other hand, have been shown to be more sensitive to dopamine, which the brain closely associates with rewards.[40] This may explain why they are more prone to ambition and achievement, things that are rewarded by others. It may also explain why they tend to seek out more pleasurable activities outside of themselves, including activities with greater social interaction, physical activity, and excitement.

---

[38] Johnson, DL; Wiebe, JS; Gold, SM; Andreasen, NC; Hichwa, RD; Watkins, GL; Boles Ponto, LL (1999). "Cerebral blood flow and personality: A positron emission tomography study". The American Journal of Psychiatry. 156 (2): 252-7. PMID 9989562.

[39] Forsman, L.J., de Manzano, O., Karabanov, A., Madison, G. & Ullen, F. (2012) Differences in regional brain volume related to the extraversion-introversion dimension—a voxel based morphometry study. Neuroscience Research, 72(1), 59-67

[40] Depue, RA; Collins, PF (1999). "Neurobiology of the structure of personality: Dopamine, facilitation of incentive motivation, and extraversion". The Behavioral and Brain Sciences. 22 (3):491-517; discussion 518-69. doi:10.1017/S0140525X9900206. PMID 11301519.

Have we uncovered all the differences between introvert and extravert brains?

Probably not. As methods of measuring brain structure and activity get more sophisticated, we will undoubtedly learn more. But the fact remains, there are physical differences in introvert and extravert brains.

So introversion is not all "in our heads"...it's also in our brains.

Chapter 6: Do Introverts Think Differently?

Considering how many theories and models there are dealing with the cognitive processes of introverts and extraverts, there are surprisingly few studies that actually look into how introverts think.

Introverts respond more quickly to all stimuli, but more slowly to changes. One such study was designed to examine college undergraduate students who had either scored high or low on a questionnaire on extraversion.[41] The researchers had the students view computer screens which presented sets of colored squares, with each set showing either 2, 4, or 6 different colors. The colors of the squares changed 50% of the time. The students were hooked up to an electroencephalogram (EEG) to measure the response times of their brains to the different sets of the squares.

Interestingly enough, the introverts in the study had brains which reacted more strongly to all incoming stimuli (shown on their EEGs as larger initial peaks), whether the colors of the squares changed or didn't. The EEGs showed that the introverts also studied the stimuli more deeply. When it came to reacting to changes in the colors of the squares, the extraverts showed greater reactivity.

The researchers concluded that the extraverts were more sensitive to changes in their surroundings than the introverts. Introverts reacted more slowly and with less intensity to environmental changes.

The most interesting part of this study was that it showed, by measuring brain activity, that there was a physical difference in the brains of introverts and extraverts when responding to the same set of stimuli.

It also may explain why introverts need alone time, why they find social settings to be draining, and why they are slow to react, in general: *introvert brains are literally reacting more quickly and more intensely to any and all information coming in.*

No wonder introverts need to get away from it all in order to recharge.

---

[41] Stauffer, C. C., Indermuhle, R., Troche, S. J., & Rammsayer, T.H. (2012). Extraversion and short-term memory for chromatic stimuli: An event-related potential analysis. *International Journal of Psychophysiology*, 86, 66-73. doi: 10.1016/j.ijpsycho.2012.07.184

Chapter 7: How Do Introverts Behave Differently?

Studies into the behavior of introverts are still in the early stages. While the main goal for understanding introverts and extraverts may arguably be so that we can understand how they behave differently, there hasn't been as much research into how introverts and extraverts behave differently. There have, however, been several studies into a few specific areas where introverts and extraverts behave differently.

They dress differently. One study demonstrated that introverts preferred comfort while extraverts preferred decorative clothing.[42]

They listen to different music. Another study found that introverts preferred less upbeat, less energetic, and more unconventional music than extraverts.[43]

They party less. A study found that extraverts tended to consume alcohol more, be more popular, attend parties, date a wider variety of people, and exercise more than introverts.[44]

They talk less and spend less time with people. In perhaps the least surprising results of all time, one study found that extraverts talk more and spend more time with other people, while introverts talk less and spend less time with other people.[45] The study, which was dubbed the "Big EAR study" because of its use of miniature Electronically Activated Recorders (EARs) programmed to periodically record random snippets of sound from the study's subjects, provided a sample of the subjects' daily sounds, including conversation. The sound samples recorded by the EARs revealed that extraverts engaged in conversation more frequently than introverts.[46]

---

[42] Sharma, R. S. (1980). "Clothing behavior, personality, and values: A correlational study". *Psychological Studies*. **25** (2): 137–42.

[43] Rentfrow, Peter J.; Gosling, Samuel D. (2003). "The do re mi's of everyday life: The structure and personality correlates of music preferences". *Journal of Personality and Social Psychology*. 84 (6): 1236–56. doi:10.1037/0022-3514.84.6.1236. PMID 12793587.

[44] Paunonen, S.V. (2003). Big five factors of personality and replicated predictions of behavior. *Journal of Personality and Social Psychology*, 84(2), 411-422.

[45] Mehl, M.R. & Pennebaker, J.W. (2003). The sounds of social life: A psychometric analysis of students' daily social environments and natural conversations. *Journal of Personality and Social Psychology*, 84(4), 857-870.

[46] Mehl, M. R., Pennebaker, J. W., Crow, M. D., Dabbs, J., & Price, J. H. (2001). The Electronically Activated Recorder (EAR): A device for sampling naturalistic daily activities and conversations. *Behavior Research Methods, Instruments, and Computers, 33*, 517-523.

They even decorate their offices differently. Another study showed that introverts didn't decorate their offices as much as extraverts, who tended to decorate in order to encourage visitors to interact with them.[47]

On the Other Hand… In spite of these studies, a larger analysis suggested that introverts and extraverts do not behave all that differently. Researchers conducted a meta-analysis of 15 different studies in which subjects both answered personality questionnaires and reported their own behavior several times per day. The objective was to determine whether the personality traits indicated by the questionnaire results—including introversion/extraversion—would predict the behavior of the subjects as they went about their daily routines.

The results varied. Both introverts and extraverts acted in the opposite manner at several points throughout the day, which meant that introverts know how to behave like extraverts and did so, and vice versa. The study also showed that extraverts acted extraverted only about 5-10% more than introverts.[48]

---

[47] Gosling, S. (2008). *Snoop*. New York: Basic Books.

[48] Fleeson, W.; Gallagher, P. (2009). "The Implications of Big Five Standing for the Distribution of Trait Manifestation in Behavior: Fifteen Experience-Sampling Studies and a Meta-Analysis". *Journal of Personality and Social Psychology*. 87 (6): 1097–1114. doi:10.1037/a0016786.

Chapter 8: Are Introverts Less Happy Than Extraverts?

Perhaps the most fascinating field of study regarding introversion and extraversion is the study into how they relate to happiness.

Extraverts Are Happier

According to the research, extraverts are happier...according to extraverts.[49] Extraverts reported that they have high levels of happiness, while introverts reported lower levels of happiness. Study after study has supported this conclusion, so the connection between extraverts and higher levels of happiness is generally accepted.

In fact, the authors of one article concluded that extraversion was one of the best predictors for happiness.[50]

But why? Is it because extraverts tend to have higher self-esteem, higher confidence in social settings, and may be more optimistic than introverts? Or is it because extraverts are oblivious to, and introverts are more sensitive to, the storms raging within the deepest chambers of their minds?

Possible Explanations for Why Extraverts Are Happier

Extraverts are more optimistic. For starters, it is easier to feel happy when you tend to be more optimistic about life. A 2006 study found that extraverts judged neutral events more optimistically than introverts.[51] And extraverts may even have a more rosy outlook on the future. A 2002 study found that extraverts were more likely to believe positive things would happen in the future.[52]

---

[49] Pavot, William; Diener, Ed; Fujita, Frank. (1990). "Extraversion and happiness." *Personality and Individual Differences*. 11(12):1299-306. doi:10.1016/0191-8869(90)90157-M

[50] Diener, Ed; Suh, Eunkook M; Lucas, Richard E; Smith, Heidi L. (1999). "Subjective well-being: Three decades of progress." *Psychological Bulletin*. 125(2):276-302. doi: 10:1037/0033-2909.125.2.276

[51] Uziel, L. (2006). The extraverted and the neurotic glasses are of different colors. *Personality and Individual Differences*, 41(4), 745-754.

[52] Zelenski, J.M., & Larsen, R.J. (2002). Predicting the future: How affect-related personality traits influence likelihood judgments of future events. *Personality and Social Psychology Bulletin*, 28(7), 1000-1010.

Extraverts have higher levels of self-esteem. More than one study has demonstrated that extraverts have higher levels of self-esteem than introverts [53], which is an important component of happiness.

It may take less to make extraverts happy. Different lines of research have explored whether it just takes less to make extraverts happier than it does for introverts. One theory is that extraverts have a lower threshold for happiness than introverts, so it takes less to get extraverts to happy. The other theory is that extraverts just react more strongly to positive events than introverts, leading them to react with more happiness to events than introverts do. Some aspects of both theories were supported by a 1998 study[54], but there may be other dimensions of personality (neuroticism, for example) that also affect the levels of happiness extraverts feel.

Extraverts may be happier because they tend to do more of what they love. Extraverts seek out social situations more than introverts do, and extraverts tend be happier in social situations than introverts. This is what common sense (and the social activity hypothesis) would tell us is one reason extraverts are happier. But is it accurate?

Some studies support this idea: extraverts are more sociable, and they also get more happiness from being sociable.[55] But other studies have shown that there isn't really much of a difference in how much time introverts and extraverts spend being social, and that introverts felt just as much happiness from social interactions.[56]

Having said that, being social is more of an effort for introverts. And since everyone has to have social interactions with the people around them on a daily basis as a fact of life, it is possible that introverts find it more stressful to be social and this lowers their level of happiness.

Extraverts may be happier because they are predisposed to be happier. Under the "affective reactivity model," one's personality influences how strongly one reacts to positive or negative events. Consequently, extraverts, who typically

---

[53] Cheng, Helen; Furnham, Adrian (2003). "Personality, self-esteem, and demographic predictions of happiness and depression." *Personality and Individual Differences.* 34(6): 921-42. doi:10.1016/S0191-8869(02)00078-8.

[54] Gross, J.J., Sutton, S.K., and Ketelaar, T. (1998). Relations between affect and personality: Support for the affect-level and affective reactivity views. *Personality and Social Psychology Bulletin*, 24(3), 279-288.

[55] Furnham, Adrian; Brewin, Chris R. (1990). "Personality and happiness." *Personality and Individual Differences.* 11(10): 1093-6. doi:10.1016/0191-8869(90)90138-H.

[56] Pavot, William; Diener, Ed; Fujita, Frank. (1990). "Extraversion and happiness." *Personality and Individual Differences.* 11(12):1299-306. doi:10.1016/0191-8869(90)90157-M

react more to positive stimuli, are believed to have a greater predisposition to happiness, since happiness has a greater effect on them. Whereas introverts are less responsive to rewards, extraverts are more responsive to rewards and react more strongly to positive events.[57]

Extravert qualities may lead to happier circumstances. Since extraverts seek out social situations more often, it is possible that this very quality leads them to better and happier life circumstances: more parties, more friends, more dates, more promotions on the job. It is possible that these better life circumstances are the reason extraverts report higher levels of happiness.

Even Introverts Are Happier When They Act Like Extraverts

Of course, there is the possibility that extraverts are happier because of what they *do,* rather than who they *are.* Studies have tied happiness to "acting" extraverted, *regardless of whether the acting is done by introverts or extraverts.*[58]

This was duplicated in experiments where people were instructed to *act* more extraverted, regardless of how they identified themselves (introvert or extravert). This led to the conclusion that being extraverted in the moment caused happiness in the moment.[59]

So perhaps happiness is less about *being* a certain way and more about *acting* a certain way.

But Does This Mean Introverts Are Unhappy?

Of course, if extraverts tend to be happier, does this mean that introverts are unhappy?

Not necessarily.

Part of the problem may be that extraverts and introverts react differently to pleasant events. So where an extravert might feel "happy" when they are excited,

---

[57] Gable, Shelley L.; Reis, Harry T.; Elliot, Andrew J. (2000). "Behavioral activation and inhibition in everyday life." *Journal of Personality and Social Psychology.* 78(6): 1135-49. doi: 10.1037/0022-3514.78.6.1135. PMID 10870914.

[58] Fleeson, William; Malanos, Adriane B.; Achille, Noelle M. (2002). "An intraindividual process approach to the relationship between extraversion and positive affect: Is acting extraverted as 'good' as being extraverted?" *Journal of Personality and Social Psychology.* 83(6): 1409-22. doi: 10.1037/0022-3514.83.6.1409. PMID 12500821.

[59] McNiel, J. & Fleeson, W. (2006). The causal effects of extraversion on positive affect and neuroticism on negative affect: Manipulating state extraversion and state neuroticism in an experimental approach. *Journal of Research in Personality,* 40(5), 529-550.

an introvert would see a lot of excitement as unpleasant. When things are going well for an introvert, they might feel relaxed and peaceful instead.

Now, introversion has been linked in some studies with mood disorders, specifically depression and anxiety. But while there may be a correlation between emotionally unstable introverts and depression or anxiety[60], it is also true that emotionally stable introverts aren't any more vulnerable to depression and anxiety than emotionally stable extraverts.

And happiness with life can be affected by a large number of things that have nothing to do with introversion or extraversion: the tendency to be emotionally stable versus being neurotic. Whether an individual has a strong sense of themselves (as a whole personality, not just as an introvert or extravert). Or even growing up and living in a culture that is more or less happy.

So to be an introvert does not necessarily mean you are condemned to a life of unhappiness. On the contrary, introverts can be just as happy as extraverts. We just have a different way of feeling, and expressing, happiness.

---

[60] Krueger, R.F., Caspi, A., Moffitt, T.E., Silva, P.A. & McGee, R. (1996). "Personality traits are differentially linked to mental disorders: A multitrait-multidiagnosis study of an adolescent birth cohort. *Journal of Abnormal Psychology*, 105(3), 299-312.

Chapter 9: Introverts In The Real World

It is one thing to review the different personality models, or the scientific theories and research studies on introversion and extraversion.

But introverts have to live in the real world.

In fact, introverts often have to live in a world that favors and rewards extraverts. We have all heard the expression "the squeaky wheel gets the grease." Well, it is also true that the assertive employee gets the raise, the sociable salesperson gets the sale, the loudest message gets the attention.

And the introverts, who often live and work quietly, neither motivated by outside praise nor seeking it, are often ignored or overlooked. At work. In social settings. In relationships.

However, introverts bring special qualities to the table that balance out extravert tendencies. And they can use these qualities—their introvert strengths—to not just survive, but thrive, even in an extravert-dominated culture.

In this chapter, we'll look at the sizeable list of well-known introverts who have achieved success, past and present.

We will also take a look at the strengths—ones available to all introverts—that successful introverts use to succeed, and explore how introverts run into problems.

Finally, we will take a look at how introverts can use their unique qualities to succeed in life.

A Short List of Famously Successful Introverts

A short list of successful introverts, past and present, includes:

Abraham Lincoln – The 16th president of the United States. Known for being quiet and reserved (but not above telling jokes), he may be responsible for the fact that the United States still exists, as he presided over the Civil War, determined to keep the Union intact.

Al Gore – Former Vice President of the United States and climate change activist. Despite being in the public eye, first as a politician, then as the voice of the climate change movement, Gore is considered an introvert. He has been quoted as saying:

> "Most people in politics draw energy from backslapping and shaking hands and all that. I draw energy from discussing ideas."[61]

Albert Einstein – Physicist. The father of the Theory of Relativity was well-known for his ability to think deeply. He was also clearly an introvert. As he said of himself:

> "I am truly a 'lone traveler' and have never belonged to my country, my home, my friends, or even my immediate family, with my whole heart; in the face of all these ties, I have never lost a sense of distance and a need for solitude."[62]

Audrey Hepburn – Movie star. Despite being an acclaimed actress who was very comfortable in front of the camera, Hepburn identified as an introvert. She said of herself:

> "I have to be alone very often. I'd be quite happy if I spent from Saturday night until Monday morning alone in my apartment. That's how I refuel."[63]

Barack Obama – President of the United States. Known for his ability to speak inspirationally to large groups of people, President Obama is also an introvert.

Bill Gates – Microsoft co-founder and multi-billionaire. No surprise that a man who started off spending hours programming in front of a computer would be an introvert.

Charles Darwin – Biologist. The man who wrote "On The Origin of Species" and promoted the Theory of Evolution might not have done so if he did not enjoy solitude and deep thought as much as he did.

Christina Aguilera – Pop star. Despite her loud and flamboyant onstage personality (and amazing voice), Christina identifies herself as being "intense and introverted."

Eleanor Roosevelt – Wife of President Franklin Delano Roosevelt and one of the most beloved first ladies of all time. Despite living a very public life and being very comfortable with the press, she once said "Friendship with oneself is all important, because without it one cannot be friends with anyone else in the world."

---

[61] http://introvertspring.com/top-100-introvert-quotes/

[62] Einstein, Albert. *The World As I See It*. Citadel Press Books (1956).

[63] http://introvertspring.com/top-100-introvert-quotes/

Fredric Chopin – Composer. World-famous for his compositions, Chopin gave very few public performances.

George Stephanopoulos – Political Advisor and TV Host. Despite being in the public eye since his early days as a political advisor to President Bill Clinton, Stephanopoulos has claimed publicly that he is an introvert.

Guy Kawasaki – The influential executive at Apple during the 1980s and author has claimed he is an introvert.

Hillary Clinton – Former First Lady, Secretary of State and, at the time of this writing, 2016 presidential candidate. Unlike her husband, former President Bill Clinton, Hillary Clinton is not extraverted.

J.K. Rowling – Author of the Harry Potter series of books, among others. It is no surprise that the famous novelist is an introvert, as writing novels frequently requires deep thinking and solitary writing time.

Mahatma Gandhi – Indian political and social leader. The man who invented civil disobedience and worked tirelessly for human rights in India was also an introvert. Gandhi once famously said:

> "In a gentle way, you can shake the world."[64]

Mark Zuckerberg – CEO of Facebook. Despite revolutionizing social media through his invention of Facebook, Zuckerberg is known for being reserved with those he doesn't know.

Meryl Streep – Actress. Possibly the most decorated movie actress in US history, Streep is also an introvert.

Rosa Parks – Civil rights icon. The woman who refused to give up her bus seat to a white man on a bus in Montgomery Alabama in 1955 was often described as quiet, gentle, and soft-spoken.

Roy Rogers – Singer, Actor. The man who made many movies as the singing cowboy said of himself "I am an introvert at heart."

Sir Isaac Newton – Scientist. The man who conceived of the laws of motion, universal gravitation, and thermodynamics was a deeply private introvert.

Steve Wozniak – Co-founder of Apple. He is famously quoted as saying the following:

---

[64] http://introvertspring.com/top-100-introvert-quotes/

"I don't believe anything really revolutionary has ever been invented by committee…I'm going to give you some advice that might be hard to take…Work alone…

Most inventors and engineers I've met are like me. They're shy and they live in their heads. The very best of them are artists. And artists work best alone."[65]

Steven Spielberg – Movie director. Possibly the most well-known and successful movie director in American cinema, Spielberg is an admitted introvert.

Warren Buffett – The famed investor and multi-billionaire is known for his ability to carefully think about investing in circumstances where others might panic.

As you can see from this short list of successful introverts, being an introvert is no barrier to success and achievement. In fact, in some cases (for example, being an author), it may even be a requirement!

It is also interesting to note that, even among this short list of famous introverts, certain careers keep popping up. There are the kind of careers where you would expect that solitude and focus to be necessary, such as scientists and computer programmers. You also find careers that require creativity and self-awareness, such as authors, musicians, and actors. And, perhaps surprisingly, you even find a few political and social leaders.

---

[65] http://introvertspring.com/top-100-introvert-quotes/

Chapter 10: What Characteristics Do Successful Introverts Have In Common?

While introverted qualities tend to get downplayed in our extravert-dominated society, there are several characteristics that successful introverts have in common:

Deep Personal Relationships. Introverts do not tend to have many superficial relationships, as extraverts do. They tend to have fewer but deeper and more meaningful relationships. While introverts are not the easiest people to get to know, they are very comfortable with people they already know. Introverts tend to prize and cultivate their close relationships.

Independence. Introverts prefer working independently. They can also work with minimal supervision and can be alone without difficulty.

Deep Thinking. Introverts tend more towards quiet contemplation, which facilitates deep thinking, creativity, and consistently coming up with innovative ideas.

Intensity and Focus. Introverts can focus intensely on the task at hand.

Empathy and Emotional Sensitivity. Introverts show greater emotional sensitivity.

Team Contributors. Introverts can be good followers, allowing others to lead. This makes introverts great team players.

Work Ethic. Introverts don't feel the need to trumpet their accomplishments or their thoughts. They just want to get the job done.

Restraint. Introverts tend to show more restraint than introverts in social settings. This leads to fewer social gaffes, fewer "foot-in-mouth" episodes, and a deeper sense of what is appropriate for a given situation.

Slow to React. Because introverts tend to react slowly, they have less of a tendency to make rash mistakes due to moving too quickly.

Pleasant Company. Introverts can be nicer to be around because they tend to be laid-back, low-key, and unaggressive.

Preference for Routine. Introverts prefer steadiness and routine, which can be a bonus when working on projects which require repetition and perseverance.

These aren't the only qualities that successful introverts have. In fact, you can expand or condense the list significantly. For example, a *Fast Company* article listed the following "4 Traits of Introverts That Make Them Great Leaders"[66]:

1. Listening Skills
2. Deep Thinking
3. A Calming Presence
4. Preparedness

Introverts, therefore, possess a number of qualities that they can use to serve others and to succeed.

---

[66] https://www.fastcompany.com/3051624/lessons-learned/4-traits-of-introverts-that-make-them-great-leaders

Chapter 11: Where Can Things Get Problematic for Introverts in a Social Society?

Some of the same characteristics that can make introverts more pleasant to be around, can also impede their advancement. In a society that values assertiveness and drive, introverts can quickly find themselves pushed out of the way when it comes to promotions at work, social and networking activities, or even meeting their basic daily needs.

Deep Personal Relationships. This becomes a problem introverts because they can be hard to get to know. Modern society requires daily social interaction with others, from loved ones to coworkers to the checkout person at the corner drugstore. Such daily activities, including the networking necessary for business and career success, requires the ability to be comfortable forming and cultivating casual, superficial relationships.

Independence. Introverts prefer working independently, but this may not always be possible. Businesses often run on interactions between and among teams, forcing introverts to work with others, a situation they may not be comfortable with.

Deep Thinking. While creativity and innovation are prized in some careers (such as the arts, or research & development), the preference for introverts to go deep may keep them from taking needed action.

Intensity and Focus. While introverts like to focus on the task at hand until it is done, there is no doubt that we live in a world full of interruptions and distractions that will leave many introverts feeling frustrated. Many workplaces favor a multi-tasking, project-based approach that may not play to introvert strengths.

Empathy and Emotional Sensitivity. While introverts may show greater sensitivity to others' emotions, this tendency may leave them vulnerable to emotionally needy people who demand their attention.

Comfortable with Following. While introverts make great followers, they must also be comfortable in the role of leader if they want to advance in whatever their chosen profession is.

Work Ethic. Introverts may just want to get the job done, without feeling the need to call any attention to their achievements. This may leave them overlooked in a culture where only the workers who "toot their own horns" are rewarded for their accomplishments.

Restraint. Introverts tend to show more restraint. This may, however, lead to lost opportunities to communicate and connect with others.

Slow to React. Similarly, because introverts tend to be slow to react, they may also be slow to take necessary risks, make decisions, take actions, or jump at fleeting opportunities.

Pleasant Company. As discussed earlier, introverts may be pleasantly laid-back, low-key, and unaggressive. While this quality has its benefits, it may also leave them open to being taken advantage of by more aggressive individuals seeking to impose their agendas on others.

Preference for Routine. The introvert preference for routine can become a stumbling block for them. Introverts looking for routine may be unable to deal with surprises or rapidly changing conditions.

Other Ways Introverts Can Get Themselves Into Trouble

Introverts can have difficulties as Entrepreneurs and Business Owners: Beth L. Buelow, author of "The Introvert Entrepreneur," stated in an interview with *Psychology Today*[67] that introvert entrepreneurs faced challenges specific to introverts:

- Effective networking
- Selling without feeling like they were being "salesy"
- Standing out in a "loud marketplace"

Buelow pointed out that successful businesses need *people*: as customers, as employees, as business partners, and as components of a community. While introverts tend to, as she said, "default to lone-ranger status," it is difficult to succeed in business this way.

Introverts can have difficulties understanding extravert coworkers: Two different studies highlighted the fact that introverts tend to judge their extravert team members rather harshly.[68] [69] Professor Keith Leavitt, one of the co-authors

---

[67] https://www.psychologytoday.com/blog/self-promotion-introverts/201606/introverts-secrets-running-successful-business

[68] http://www.huffingtonpost.com/2014/12/17/introverts-workplace_n_6341204.html

[69] Amir Erez, Pauline Schilpzand, Keith Leavitt, Andrew H. Woolum, and Timothy A. Judge (2015). Inherently Relational: Interactions between Peers' and Individuals' Personalities Impact Reward Giving and Appraisal of Individual Performance *Academy of Management Journal*. 58:6 1761-1784. doi:10.5465/amj.2011.0214

of both studies, said that introverts could also have trouble concentrating in noisy offices or anywhere where stimulation is high. "Extraverts tend to be 'high stimulus' people," Leavitt said. "By talking loudly, passionately, and frequently, they quickly overwhelm their introverted teammates.'" Introverts, therefore, value certain personality traits (their own) and may be hypersensitive to extravert qualities.

Chapter 12: So How Can Introverts Win?

Given that the very qualities that make introverts unique can also become stumbling blocks for them, how can introverts ever succeed in an extravert's society?

Coping With Introversion in the Workplace

As mentioned in the last chapter, modern workplaces are hard on introverts. Offices are often noisy and sometimes far more open than introverts would like. Add meetings, phone calls, constant interruptions, and expected socialization with coworkers, and you have an environment that is far too stimulating for introverts.

So how is an introvert to survive in an extravert workplace?

Here are a few possibilities:

1. *Try to find a quiet space.* If you are in an office with too many distractions, try to find a spot farther from the noise, or a place where you can close the door.

2. *Use communication tools that play to your strengths.* Thinking on your feet and reacting quickly are required when you make phone calls or have face-to-face meetings. But e-mail is perfect for a slower, more well-thought-out message.

3. *Lobby for a work-from-home arrangement.* If it is impossible to work well in your office as it is now, suggest to your supervisor an arrangement where you can work from home. Technology has come a long way in allowing workers to stay connected, even from home. Before discussing with your boss, figure out how you can track and measure your productivity, then compare the results from your work-from-home days with your office days. If the results show that you're more productive at home versus in the office, discuss the results with your boss and use them to support your case for a work-from-home arrangement.

Ways that Technology Is Playing to Introvert Strengths

First, came the cell phone and voicemail. Then e-mail and instant messaging apps. We now have online networking, online dating, online courses, and webinars. Cloud computing has made it possible for employees, entrepreneurs, and freelancers to work remotely from home.

It is a golden age for introverts, who can communicate and work with others while largely avoiding the disruptive socializing that necessarily accompanied a brick-and-mortar workplace. Technology has turned social interaction into something introverts can stomach and even enjoy.

On top of that, we live in the age of social media. A quick look at the numbers will reveal that social media sites are unbelievably popular and have huge memberships[70]:

Facebook	1.5 billion users
YouTube	1 billion users
Twitter	313 million users
LinkedIn	400 million users
Instagram	77 million users

And these are just a few of the social networks currently available to Internet users. There are so many others: Pinterest, Snapchat, Tumblr, Reddit, Google+, WhatsApp, and many, many more. In fact, an estimated 78% of the population of the United States subscribes to at least one social network.

And this is not just an American phenomenon. Worldwide, there are estimated to be 2.34 billion social network users.[71]

Despite the fact that social media seem custom-made for oversharing, superficiality, and constant connectedness (all of which introverts intensely dislike), it turns out that social media perfectly suits introverts and plays to their strengths.

One study on the use of social media by introverts and extraverts found that while extraverts posted more often to Facebook, introverts spent more time on the social media website.[72] Why would introverts spend more time on *social* media when they dislike being social? The simple answer: *control*.

Social media sites like Facebook allow introverts to control who they interact with online and when they interact online. They can easily block people or simply log off when the social interaction becomes too draining. In addition, because social media sites are primarily websites where you can post written thoughts in the form of status updates and comments, they play to introvert strengths of observing the thread of the online conversation, thinking deeply about it, considering how they will react to it, and responding through the written word.

---

[70] http://www.makeuseof.com/tag/12-social-media-facts-statistics-know-2016/

[71] http://www.smartinsights.com/social-media-marketing/social-media-strategy/new-global-social-media-research/

[72] Sheldon, P. (2009). "'I'll poke you. You'll poke me!' Self-disclosure, social attraction, predictability and trust as important predictors of Facebook relationships," *Cyberpsychology: Journal of Psychosocial Research on Cyberspace*,3(2), Article 1.

Social media is unquestionably here to stay. Their continued existence, coupled with the constant creation of new outlets for online communication, offers introverts unique opportunities to use this passive form of interaction as a vehicle for social and professional advancement.

Chapter 13: What Does The Future Hold for Introverts?

Given all we have discussed in this book, you would think that the future for introverts in an increasingly extraverted world would be dim.

On the contrary, the number of successful, high-achieving people who are considered introverts is astounding. Many of these people are in high-profile careers, despite their introversion.

While we do live in a world that often rewards extraverts for being extraverts, we have seen that introverts can succeed even in an extravert-dominated workplace, with its open cubicles and focus on teamwork and networking.

And technology has actually evolved to the point where it is making it easier to succeed as an introvert in an extravert world. The widespread use of the internet and cloud computing has powered the way for less confrontational forms of commerce, like remote work and the gig economy, both of which play to introvert strengths of independence, self-motivation, and focus.

The rise of social media also favors the introvert. You would think the ability to broadcast your thoughts to the world 24/7 would be an introvert's worst nightmare, but it actually plays to the introvert's strengths of deep thinking and writing.

Of course, being an introvert is no obstacle to creativity or success. While our world is becoming increasingly more connected, there will always be a need for deep thinkers, creatives, visionaries, and leaders who react not from impulse but from a position of consideration and understanding.

And with the increased attention paid in recent years to the definition of introversion, public appreciation for introverts and their unique qualities is at an all-time high, and rising.

Chapter 14: Can Society Change? Can Introverts Change? And Should They?

Given the general disconnect between the types of personality traits our society rewards and those held by introverts, it is natural to wonder how we might bring about change in order to reconcile the conflict. Will society have to change to accommodate its introverts? Or will introverts have to change to accommodate society? Is it possible for introverts to change? And if so, should they?

Can Society Change?

American culture is filled with nostalgic themes, concepts, and attitudes that have been revered for generations:

The work ethic of the Protestants.
The boldness of the pioneer.
The individualism of the cowboy.
The hustle of the middle-class family reaching for the American Dream.
The glamour of the movie star and the celebrity athlete.
The charisma of the confident, assertive, vocal leaders.

American culture, where we are all raised to believe we can rise from rags to riches through sheer determination, assertiveness, boldness, risk-taking, and networking, clearly exalts the extraverts among us.

But is America really a homogeneous nation of extraverts? A 13-year study headed by British psychologist Jason Rentfrow found that different regions of the U.S. had different personalities. According to the study, the Midwest and the South scored highest for sociability and agreeability (i.e., extraversion). The Northeastern states were more inhibited, the Western states more relaxed.[73]

However, even though the study found some regions to be more extraverted than others, a cursory glance at the numbers, state by state, shows that the majority of states score at 50 or above on extraversion. That is a majority of states leaning more towards extraversion than introversion.

Overall, the data suggest that the United States is an extraverted society, and the trait runs deep, even when you look at the data state by state. Given the prevalence of extraversion in our national identity, the characterization of America as a nation of extraverts is unlikely to change.

---

[73] http://www.dailymail.co.uk/news/article-2473707/Where-U-S-live-Graphic-shows-state-matches-personality.html

Can Introverts Change?

If society cannot and will not change, where does that leave introverts? Can they change, or should they expect to be forever relegated to second-class citizenship?

While introversion can sometimes seem like a trait that is set in stone, there is evidence that introverts *can* change over time.

A study of 2,000 people conducted over a 15-year period demonstrated that personality can change, even in adults over 30.[74]

As discussed in Chapter 2, researchers Costa and McCrae, who refined the "Big 5" personality traits to measure 6 facets for each trait, showed that introverts who took the same test over several years, would yield different personality traits over time, which points to the fact that personality is a lot more fluid than we tend to believe.

Over the course of a lifetime, all people change, and the introverts among us are no different. As introverts get older and understand themselves and the world better, they also tend to become warmer, more communicative, more assertive, more risk-taking, and more expressive, just as extraverts may become quieter, more contemplative, less aggressive, less active, and more thoughtful. Not only do we change naturally as we age, but we can also take steps to deliberately cultivate other qualities.

So yes. It is possible for introverts to change. But should they?

Should Introverts Change?

In a society that values extravert qualities, it's easy to see why introversion would be viewed negatively, as something in need of change or repair.

But introverts bring qualities to the table that offer a much-needed social balance.

Without introverts, we might not have literature or art. Without introverts, we might not have invention and innovation. Without introverts, we might not have technological advances and scientific exploration. Without introverts, we might not have analytical problem-solvers and thoughtful counselors.

Without introverts to counterbalance the surplus of outwardly-directed, extraverted energy in our society, we might not have the inner strength and self-knowledge to advance. Society might be busy and active and social without them,

---

[74] Terraciano, A, McCrae, R. R., Brant, L.J., & Costa, P. R. (2005). Hierarchical linear modeling analyses of the NEO-PI-R Scales in the Baltimore Longitudinal Study of Aging. *Psychology and Aging*, 20(3), 493-506. doi:10.1037/0082-7974.20.3.493)

but it would suffer in the absence of the quiet significance that introverts bring forth from within themselves and bestow upon the world.

Should introverts adapt to specific social situations? Perhaps. They could certainly benefit from being more extraverted under certain circumstances. But introverts should never give up the essence of what makes them special and unique, because even though society might underappreciate them, we all benefit from introverts being who they are.

Conclusion

The study of introverts has a long and interesting history, and the psychological theories on introversion, including theories on what causes it and how we can measure it, continue to develop. Without a doubt, research has a long way to go before it fully and completely unmasks why we are who we are.

Research to date, however, has certainly given us a deeper understanding of the ways in which introverts are different, from their genes to their brains to their levels of happiness. The research, coupled with the recent public interest in introverts, has led to a greater awareness of the differences between introverts and extraverts, and how each personality type interacts with the world.

We live in an extraverted world. Introverts nonetheless bring unique strengths to the table, and can be found among our society's most elite scientists, artists, geniuses, businessmen, and political leaders.

With the rise of technology and social media, it is possible now more than ever for introverts to be more "social," but in a way that is more accommodating, and that plays to their strengths of passivity, control, and self-comfort.

Introverts have their place in American society. Introversion is not a disadvantage, nor is it an advantage. It is a necessary ingredient vital to America's social, economic, and political innovations. Introversion offers rationality as an antidote to the recklessness of passion, and promotes humility where ego would otherwise prevail. It is not the solution, nor is it the problem. It should not be abused or eradicated. Extraverts are also necessary, to be sure, but society has plenty of them. Introversion, therefore, is *balance*: we can choose to either stand tall underneath it, or perish in its absence.

Printed in Great Britain
by Amazon